Ten Poem
Husbands a

ex libris

Candlestick Press

Published by:
Candlestick Press,
Diversity House, 72 Nottingham Road, Arnold, Nottingham UK NG5 6LF
www.candlestickpress.co.uk

Design and typesetting by Craig Twigg

Printed by Ratcliff & Roper Print Group, Nottinghamshire, UK

Selection © Di Slaney and Katharine Towers, 2019

Cover illustration © Hilke MacIntyre 2019
www.macintyre-art.com

Candlestick Press monogram © Barbara Shaw, 2008

© Candlestick Press, 2019
Reprinted 2021, 2022, 2023

ISBN 978 1 907598 81 4

Acknowledgements:

The poems in this pamphlet are reprinted from the following books, all by permission of the publishers listed unless stated otherwise. Every effort has been made to trace the copyright holders of the poems published in this book. The editor and publisher apologise if any material has been included without permission or without the appropriate acknowledgement, and would be glad to be told of anyone who has not been consulted. Thanks are due to all the copyright holders cited below for their kind permission:

Moniza Alvi, *Split World: Poems 1990-2005* (Bloodaxe Books, 2005) www.bloodaxebooks.com. Tiffany Atkinson, *Catulla et al* (Bloodaxe Books, 2011) www.bloodaxebooks.com. Mike Barlow, *Another Place* (Salt, 2007) by kind permission of the author. Angela Carter, *Unicorn: The Poetry of Angela Carter* (Profile Books, 2015) by kind permission of Rogers, Coleridge and White. Choman Hardi, *Considering the Women* (Bloodaxe Books, 2015) www.bloodaxebooks.com. Paul Henry, *Ingrid's Husband* (Seren, 2007). Ada Limon, *The Carrying* (Milkweed Editions, 2008). Linda Pastan, *Carnival Evening: New and Selected Poems 1968 – 1998* (W. W. Norton, 1999) Copyright © 1999 by Linda Pastan. Used by permission of W. W. Norton & Company, Inc. All rights reserved. RS Thomas, *Selected Poems 1948 – 1968* (Bloodaxe Books, 1986) www.bloodaxebooks.com. Tiphanie Yanique, *Wife* (Peepal Tree Press, 2015).

All permissions cleared courtesy of Swift Permissions (swiftpermissions@gmail.com).

Where poets are no longer living, their dates are given.

Contents

Portrait of the Husband as Farmers' Market

The husband is a mud-on-the-boots philosophy
in old jeans, loving nothing so much as slow growth.

His thoughts are distinctively British cooperatives,
jovial stall-holders subbing each other loose change.

His chest is a trestle laid with rare meats, smelling
of the smokehouse, his belly a seed-loaf, knotted

and oddly exotic. The sex of the husband's a plump
trout, a one-off, lolling silverside-up in its shine

for a wife with the eye of a magpie. His heart,
apparently a leafy crop, is a loom of many rhizomes

reaching furlongs – who knows how far? The husband
is mineral-rich, irregular, leaving scraps of himself

all over the street for starlings to pick at. Is a crowd
of bright skins in a bushel, wheels of feral cheese,

impossible brews from the ditches. Is the season's
measure, taking the weather however it turns out.

Tiffany Atkinson

Farm Wife

Hers is the clean apron, good for fire
Or lamp to embroider, as we talk slowly
In the long kitchen, while the white dough
Turns to pastry in the great oven,
Sweetly and surely as hay making
In a June meadow; hers are the hands,
Humble with milking, but still now
In her wide lap as though they heard
A quiet music, hers being the voice
That coaxes time back to the shadows
In the room's corners. O, hers is all
This strong body, the safe island
Where men may come, sons and lovers,
Daring the cold seas of her eyes.

RS Thomas (1913 – 2000)

To My Dear and Loving Husband

If ever two were one, then surely we.
If ever man were loved by wife, then thee;
If ever wife was happy in a man,
Compare with me ye women if you can.
I prize thy love more than whole mines of gold,
Or all the riches that the East doth hold.
My love is such that rivers cannot quench,
Nor ought but love from thee, give recompence.
Thy love is such I can no way repay,
The heavens reward thee manifold I pray.
Then while we live, in love lets so persever,
That when we live no more, we may live ever.

Anne Bradstreet (1612 – 1672)

Wife

I'm not yet comfortable with the word,
its short clean woosh that sounds like
life. At dinner last night my single girls
said in admonition, *It's not wife-approved*
about a friend's upcoming trip. Their
eyes rolled up and over and out of their
pretty young heads, Wife, why does it
sound like a job? *I want a wife,* the famous
feminist wrote, *a wife who will keep my
clothes clean, ironed, mended, replaced
when need be.* A word that could be made
easily into a maid. A wife that does, fixes,
soothes, honors, obeys. Housewife,
fishwife, bad wife, good wife, what's
the word for someone who stares long
into the morning, unable to even fix tea
some days, the kettle steaming over
loud like a train whistle, she who cries
in the mornings, she who tears a hole
in the earth and cannot stop grieving,
the one who wants to love you, but often
isn't good at even that, the one who
doesn't want to be diminished
by how much she wants to be yours.

Ada Limón

Ingrid's Husband

The roadside leaves leapt out
as if to flag me down.

I stopped for some razor-blades.
The shop assistant asked
Are you Ingrid's husband?

No. But afterwards,
all the dwindling miles,
I wondered what she was like,

Ingrid, what soap she used,
if her hair was the colour
of these crazy leaves

and if she was mad or sane
or some shade in between.

Perhaps if we met
I'd grow to love her name.

I have seen leaves migrate
to parallel lives –

blown through an underpass
from the eastern side
of a motorway to the west.

Perhaps I should have answered *Yes.*

Paul Henry

Carrying My Wife

I carried my wife inside me –
like a cable car I pulled her
up the mountainside of our days.

I lifted her quite naturally
and I carried the floating,
prancing seahorse within her.

I took them both to the crossroads.
Stooping like St Christopher
I bore her – a slippery wave.

The hospital parted for us
strongly as the Red Sea.
I coaxed her through swing doors

which gusted to and fro
like our past and future.
She was sea-sick.

Sometimes she could hardly
remember who I was.
I only intended to leave her

for a moment in the bulrushes,
but she slept and slept,
hibernated like a star

gone to ground.
Then I carried her
to the ends of the Earth.

Moniza Alvi

The Seventh Wedding Invitation

Dear friends and family,
I promise this will be my last wedding
if it doesn't work out, I will just live with
another man, no more pledges. So please
come along to this final ceremony with a man
who, at the moment, fills my eyes. Do not
bring any more presents – pura Shahla's
non-stick pan is still in the box. Mama Hama's
gold ring has not been put on. And the naughty
lingerie will be worn for this man since my ex
was orthodox. He did not last. Do come along.
I promise to wear something more sophisticated
than a wedding dress. It is another chance to meet
and talk about Ama's failure in bringing up
her children, to shed light, one more time,
on Layla's divorce, and Nina's remarriage
to her brother in law. We will have a fun night.
I have told my new man so much about you
and it may be your only chance to meet him.
With all my love, your little Lala.

Choman Hardi

The Third Wife

My first wife knew no more than me, no telling
where her needs ended, mine began. One day though
I turned the hill to find the boat moored in the field,
the house out in the bay, adrift, door open wide.
I rowed out to a message on the mat: gone
to my cousin's place in Valparaiso.

My second wife blew ashore in a force ten
leading a shipload of apprentices astray
with her white dress, her turned-up Nordic nose,
her precious bible clutched in a manicured hand.
No matter how I pumped, the organ of her heart played flat,
her painted smile as wooden as a figurehead's.

My third wife won't say where she lives.
She comes to me when the tides are right,
stays longer if a wind's got up or fog's come down.
I stroke the warm loaves of her biceps, kiss
dimpled elbows, listen for the souch
our breathing makes when we're together.

She has cousins everywhere. They post her money
in denominations the local shop won't take
or drop by uninvited while we're having tea. They push me
into corners, whisper her address. I turn a deaf ear.
This is my third wife I explain, who's known
many husbands, some worse some better than me.

Mike Barlow

The Husband Speaks from the Mountain

Not from the mountain, in reality.
Metaphysically, I speak from the bush. Or the desert.
Or something on that level.

I speak of ying and yang. Husband and wife.
Except that, epistemologically, wife only means woman.
See, it's not about a partnership. There's the mistake
in our human thinking:
that we have separate thinking.
Meta-really,
we are one body, mind and all.
But see. Right there? When I do that? That's what I mean.
I felt that. I feel you.

Queen, listen. I know I'm no walk in the park.
Never have been.
But marriage isn't about
courting or canting.
I'm carrying you.
You're pushing me. I'm
not ever
going to let you fall.
Feel that? Feel me?

Even the first of my kind
had his Erin. You
see what I'm saying here?
Marriage is desert. Marriage is fire.
You are my burning bush.

See, husband means the one who takes care.
It's not that thorny. Except that it's the most of everything
in the world.
See?
      Woman, we are the mountain.

Tiphanie Yanique

Self-Portrait

after Adam Zagajewski

I am child to no one, mother to a few,
wife for the long haul.
On fall days I am happy
with my dying brethren, the leaves,
but in spring my head aches
from the flowery scents.
My husband fills a room with Mozart
which I turn off, embracing
the silence as if it were an empty page
waiting for me alone to fill it.
He digs in the black earth
with his bare hands. I scrub it
from the creases of his skin, longing
for the kind of perfection
that happens in books.
My house is my only heaven.
A red dog sleeps at my feet, dreaming
of the manic wings of flushed birds.
As the road shortens ahead of me
I look over my shoulder
to where it curves back
to childhood, its white line
bisecting the real and the imagined
the way the ridgepole of the spine
divides the two parts of the body, leaving
the soft belly in the center
vulnerable to anything.
As for my country, it blunders along
as well intentioned as Eve choosing
cider and windfalls, oblivious
to the famine soon to come.
I stir pots, bury my face in books, or hold

a telephone to my ear as if its cord
were the umbilicus of the world
whose voices still whisper to me
even after they have left
their bodies.

Linda Pastan

Afterword

Poem for a Wedding Photograph (1966)

Posing for the photographer,
they stand together under a green tree
in bridal and unfamiliar clothes.
Dressed up, they are strangers to one another.
They move awkwardly, smile
the shy, nervous smiles of shipwrecked voyagers,
never met on the crowded liner till now, in the open boat,
embarking in embarrassment on a strange voyage, together,
over a strange sea. Improvise
a sail from all her satin, make a mast
out of his body. Their hands clutch, suddenly.
We have only each other. Who are we?

Under the green tree, the bride,
gift-wrapped in white. Her veil drifts in the wind,
caressing his good black suit. The shutter clicks.
They are taken. Frozen in this eternal moment, forever.
Scissored out of the fabric of their time,
an icon of marriage (like Arnolfini and his wife
in the cluttered room, with the little dog,
to signify fidelity).

In the garden, under a tree,
the first man and wife of all and ever,
in a silver frame, for life.

Angela Carter (1940 – 1992)